Favored on Purpose

By

Lajuan Whitfield

FAVORED ON PURPOSE

To order additional copies of this book,
contact:

Lajuan Whitfield
708.856.1256

FWB Publications
Columbus, Ohio

Contents

FAVORED ON PURPOSE

Introduction

It is pertinent that we understand the kind of God we

worship, the Lord Jesus Christ. Some people, as a matter

of fact, the larger chunk of Christendom sees Him as a

grey-haired, indolent and harmless God who sits too far

in the skies with angels as His deputies and hype-men,

doing His bidding simply because He is too weak to

swing into action by Himself. He is seen as a kind of God

who academically and religiously takes note of the

happenings in the world, reserved and waiting for His

appointed day to avenge all disobedience and

wrongdoing.

But very few fail to see him for who He truly is, a God

that is calculative, super-intelligent and omniscient. The

all-knowing God is eternally mindful of the minutest of

details about not just us but the entirety of creation. Because of this level of knowledge, it cannot be correct to infer that He was just idling away when it came into His Heart to embark on the project of creation. Indeed, creation and the world, in general, is the product of a studied, calculated and projected enterprise, which would be foolhardy to attribute to the evil of hedonism or idle experimentation.

Everything that has the stamping of the Lord Jesus Christ screams purpose and direction. God's enterprise is not a gamble or a game of chance; that is why it is unforgivably erroneous to attribute anything in the creation and the running's of the earth to luck or happenstance; such word has no place in the lexicon of the cosmos and its operations. From man to animals, to the solar system, to the other planets, to nature, everything- all have their pride of place in the operations of this world and the divine scheme of things.

It is somehow disheartening that a lot of individuals are yet to come to this all-important realization, and indeed, many people who lay claims to the tenets of Christianity are bereft of this understanding. This fact comes into play in our dispositions to life, and our reactions to issues especially when things do not happen our way. _A classic example would be the way we are ruled and dictated to by the material things of this world, the scramble to keep acquiring more and more of them, to the level of doing whatever it takes to have them, including the things we barely need._ This is because we are deficient of the understanding of the purpose of God for our lives, and our wants begin to be superimposed over our needs, and we fail to see that what constitutes our wants are simply tailings and gangue that are better off not ours. We thus spend a large chunk of our lives servicing vanity and all its trappings, all the while oblivious of the fact that we have actually run adrift of God's divine purpose for our lives not just as human beings, but as His children most especially. This is one of the banes of human existence and is the root cause of most conflicts and personal troubles and travails we fall into, as well as the root cause of the heartbreak and heartache that cuts short life expectancy and makes life a shaggy, chequered and mired experience on every facet.

Purpose is defined by the bookmakers as a determined intention towards an achievement or a particular end. This summarizes the entirety of God's aim of embarking on the project of creation. It was first a thought, which graduated to a Word, and the next thing was all the chain of the events that led to the bustling, activity-prone and eventful world we have today. It is interesting to note, of course, with Scriptural backing, that everything that we find in the world today is there for a particular purpose in destiny, down to the most seemingly insignificant detail like the worms. Everything that happens in the world today is happening at its correct and scripted time, like the scenes in a grand movie. The only difference is that the running time of this divine movie is thousands and thousands of years, and even Scripture can't give us the approximate time we can expect time to completely empty out into eternity, a timeless stretch which is longer than the concept of forever. We as human beings and the elements around us are all pawns in this game of chess, actors in this wonderfully scripted flick. A good example would be the chronicling of the events that have characterized the earth up to this time, which would be a good case study to exemplify this fact.

In the Bible book of Genesis, in the first chapter, we find that the earth was without form and void. Everything was chaotic and amorphous. Now, at that time, the Bible said the Spirit of God hovered over the face of the waters. At that time, He was called Elohim, meaning the Self-Existing One. He was alone and felt there was a need to manifest other attributes inherent in Himself. He thus fancied the thought of creating things to fill up the earth that was shapeless and without meaning. He then began by commanding light to come up, and in seven days, there was an ordered and an organized planet, complete with everything needed to make life run smoothly, with a man to oversee the affairs of the garden he had created, as well as animals to keep him company. He had thus manifested His attribute as a Creator.

A simple view of all that He had created confirmed His ingenuity and intelligence, and He congratulated Himself for a job well done. But other attributes were in Him, rearing to be manifested. After creating Adam, He needed to create a woman. When this happened, she was of a fairer and weaker gender and failed to adhere to the instruction that was handed to her husband, Adam, and *this led to the fall of man*.

What a lot of people don't know is that Eve could not just help it, and her contribution to the fall and the subsequent chaos and decadence that has characterized man ever since was all in the determinate counsel of God. This was so as to create the occasion for Him to send His son in the embodiment of a Savior, to restore man back to that estate which he lost. Every other thing that happened after that Genesis account was a buildup that would empty itself into the grand appearing of the Savior in human form, the Lord Jesus Christ known as the Son of Man. This was inclusive of the story of Abraham, and his generations down to the travails of the children of Israel, the law, the prophets, everything in its entirety. This is just a microcosm of the many attributes of God and his manner of bringing them to bear on mankind. A lot of others exist.

The core thrust of this book is to depict the fact that we are all a part of a grand design, and nothing happens by chance. This should further strengthen us in handling and take in our stride, all that comes our way, knowing that as His children, it is aimed at a purpose and a definite end. It does not matter if it is a positive or negative occurrence. Armed with this knowledge, it would be easy to fulfill the scripture which admonishes us to give thanks in everything that happens to us, regardless of the nature of it.

The Book of Romans in the Bible especially chapter 8, is one of the most relatable instances of this curated thought, where the Apostle Paul boldly says that all things work together for good to those who love God. This is with particular reference to **PEOPLE WHO LOVE**

FAVORED ON PURPOSE

GOD, even though those who don't love Him also have their part to play, even though the grand outcome may not be for good as enshrined in that Scriptural passage. The book begins with an introduction to the life of Apostle Paul and what informed the penning of the book of Romans, as well as his conversion experience. Thereafter, the virtue of confidence in our sonship and all it entails as regarding this book of Romans is explored, until the favor aspect is reached, and the underlying thought is the fact that out of all that happens to the believer, a GOOD purpose is at its undertone. Intermittently, my personal life experiences and that of others that underscore this fact are interjected.

When we have this understanding, it is thus easy to flow with our God and Christian journey becomes fascinating and inspiring. This was the core belief of the Apostles that did not count it burdensome to even pay the supreme sacrifice for the sake of the gospel, and from the Scriptures, we are confident of their final destination. It is my prayer that this piece will help as many desiring Christians as it meets in this challenging journey of faith. **Amen.**

Chapter 1

THE BACKGROUND ON THE BOOK OF ROMANS

The book of Romans is one of the richest warehouses of

the essence and evidence of the purpose of God. It is so

instructive that it came from someone of the cadre and

personality of Apostle Paul, one of the best-trained lawyers

of his time in Israel. His personal resume and achievements

as well as how qualified he was in the eyes of the law at the

time added tons to his intimidating personality, and made

the book of Romans as rich as it is, in fact, the entire

epistles as written by him shows his spiritual height as well

as his deep grounding in intellectual matters. He was the

sort of person who was connected and knowledgeable, had

all the trappings of a very intelligent lawyer, and was

respected in religious circles as well. It was little wonder that he went freely to the office of person that mattered against the Christians and was able to get a covering letter to give him persecuting rights to the children of God at the time, and he was granted without question. But all of this was before the blinding and subduing power of conversion caught up with him, right there in his *'Post of Duty'*.

The story of Apostle Paul's conversion is one that is common and concurrent with the experiences of every Bible student that has had the most casual brush with the Scriptures. He was on his way to deal with the believers at that time when he was suddenly struck by a force of blinding light. Now, as a student of the Torah, he had learned that during the days of the children of Israel, they were led by the pillar of fire by night and a pillar of cloud by the day. So, you could imagine his surprise and utter confusion at seeing the same pillar of fire he believed to have been fighting for with such gumption appearing to constitute a resistance. He fell from his horse, having being over-dazzled by the power and intensity of the spotless luminous Being. To begin with, his sight was affected because he had become temporarily blind by that experience, and the route to his conversion had begun in earnest.

After his conversion, he began to embark on a series of journeys which took him through the length and breadth of Asia Minor, where he did the work of an apostle, who is traditionally called a 'setter in order' because of his in-depth knowledge of the Scriptures not just as academically crammed and analyzed, but as inspired by the unction of the Holy Ghost. As a matter of fact, this activity of the apostle was ordained of God to be so, as exemplified in the conversation that ensued with our Lord just after the murderous Saul became the saintly Paul. The Lord appeared to Ananias, a certain believer in Damascus, and commanded him to receive Paul the apostle into his house, and when he complained of the danger of that singular act on the behest of what he had the potential and intent of doing to believers, the Lord had told him that Paul was chosen of him to bear his name before kings and Gentiles as well as the children of Israel. This thus became the foundational premise on which apostle Paul said, in as much as I am the apostle to the Gentiles, I magnify my office, not in a manner that suggests vain glory seeking, but the real truth of who and what God made me.

APOSTLESHIP THE PAULINE WAY

Apostleship the Pauline way was always a question of correctness in all its ramifications. Like the foregoing, the office of an apostle is all about setting in order by the Scriptures. There are certain criteria or manifestations that characterize the apostolic office. They include the following below and Paul's stewardship was made thus peculiar because he was ready to go the extra mile of saving both his soul and that of others. He had the following qualities:

1.   He was there for everyone

In one of his writings, he wrote that he made himself a slave to everyone. He was available on hand all the time to avail the people of his teaching, his preaching, as well as his God-given advisory talent. What is more is that he did it without charging a dime. <u>This is a particular indictment on the so-called men of God today who charge for doing God's work.</u>

He was not only on hand to dish out his divinely bestowed gifts, he was not distant from the people. He was reachable. During the day, he was sitting in his workshop dealing in tents, proving for all to see that he was divinely interrupted- he was not one who felt called because he was jobless. He was not holed up in some swanky office with a retinue of aides and assistants like pretty much what is obtainable today. He had unbelievable energy and was committed to the cause of directing and establishing God's people in the Scriptures.

2. He had open arms for everyone

Apostle Paul accommodated everybody. There is a sect of believers who believed and propagated the notion that one could not do anything to save a soul. While this is partially true, they carry the belief over the board, in living anyhow they liked. Paul was never a proponent of such belief. He was quite involved in removing biased views of Scripture. He uprooted deep-seated ignorance in the people. He was summarily everything to everyone. To the Jews, he was a Jew. He would respect their customs and laws, while at the same time uphold his views. When teaching the Jews, he would make a lot of references to the Old Testament, the Torah. When he was with the Gentiles, he would join in whatever they did. Even as Jewish as he was, he would never insist that there would be those ceremonial kinds of washing that characterized their eating. He would quote people considered to be pagans and made illustrations out of their everyday affairs like their games in his teachings. Even though the Jews abhorred the pagan lifestyles, he was able to use it to reach them with the gospel.

To whomsoever he met, he stooped low to their lifestyle to be able to reach them, and this he did expertly without offending on-looking Christians who had nascent minds.

3. He was daring

Because of his seeming talismanic style of evangelism and apostleship, he was a risk taker and it paid off well in the business of soul winning. At some point, he was seen to be

FAVORED ON PURPOSE

a little hypocritical or if you like, inconsistent. For example, he preached in Corinth that the work of God was not to be paid for, yet he received gratification from the church of the Philippians. He was also accused of dubiousness because at some time he would promise to visit, but would not turn up. His outlook was more like chameleonic, and would always be suited to the people he was around. But these were viewpoints of man though.

Because of the zeal of his office, he took an unflinching stand on doctrinal matters. He rebuked sharply his brethren Barnabas and Peter when they seem to run adrift of his accommodating examples. His mantra was simple- the love of lost souls should drive one to take risks to win them for the Kingdom's sake, even at the risk of our earthly reputation.

4. The awareness of the fact that salvation was not universal

Even as much as Paul did his best to win as many souls as he could, he was aware that despite his efforts, not all could be saved. This would be because man is a free moral agent and despite the sovereignty of God, He respects man's power of choice. Paul was well aware of this fact and preached about predestination, just as it confirmed the omniscience of God that not everyone would repent and believe the gospel. That is why some would repent, and some others would be condemned.

The full awareness of this fact made Paul a player of his part and his alone in the work of salvation. He never believed it was his fault if men were not saved. He knew that it was a kind of dual work, between the believer and his God. His was just to preach the good news and establish the same in the faith. There are actually some that cannot be saved.

    5. He made double sure of his own salvation

Just like the Israelites who were delivered from bondage and were well taken care of during the journey but succumbed to what God did not like and perished in the wilderness, Apostle Paul was careful not to fall into the same bracket. He wrote- "So that I won't preach to others and myself become a castaway." Many sects of believers believe that once a man is predestinated he cannot be lost, but it is a very slippery ground because the surest proof of who is predestinated is the man who would guard his salvation with all diligence and holy living.

He likened the Christian journey to a race after which the winner would receive a prize and encouraged believers to strive for the same prize, which is eternal life. Striving according to Paul was to keep fit spiritually.

All of these and more are some of the qualities that made Paul stand out and confirm his office as a dispensational apostle. Indeed, God could not have chosen a better candidate for that office, because Apostle Paul fitted the bill so well. This chapter is about the background of the book of Romans and what led to its penning. It would be incomplete without chronicling his missionary journeys which are critical to the book of Romans.

Shortly after the Holy Ghost fell on the disciples as promised, Paul and Barnabas were called, received the commission to preach to the uncharted territories. Recall that it was in Antioch they were first called Christians. They went to Cyprus, preaching in Salamis and Paphos, but there was not much harvest there. They then proceeded to Pamphylia, then Antioch in Pisidia, where they preached to

FAVORED ON PURPOSE

the Jews on justification by faith. Many of the Jews

believed, but on the next Sabbath, some mocked the

gospel, causing Paul to turn to the Gentiles. They thus went

to Iconium, and the city was sharply divided in opinion

concerning the gospel. Paul and Barnabas actually escaped

an assassination attempt. They proceeded to Lystra and

Derbe. It seemed that many wanted to believe, but many

from Pisidia followed them and discouraged the people

from believing. Paul was stoned and assumed to be dead.

On his recovery, he went to Derbe and preached too. They

then went back through Iconium and Lystra once again,

caring for the new converts and encouraging them against

persecution. They planted churches and installed elders. It

was time to go back to Perga and Attalia and return to

Antioch in Syria where they shared testimonies.

In the second missionary journey, it was more of a follow-

up campaign on the ones who were converted on the first

journey. John Mark was the bone of contention of a serious dispute between Paul and Barnabas, and they went separate ways, Barnabas taking John Mark to Cyprus, while Paul took Silas to follow up the Christians in Syria and Cilicia. They touched Derbe and Lystra once again, strengthening the believers there. The next stop was Phrygia and Galatia. They wanted to go to Asia but were commanded not to by the Holy Spirit. They then turned west to Troas. It was here they received the Macedonian call to go to Greece and environs. This took them to Philippi where Lydia was the first convert. There was a massive success, and the people were so angry that they had Paul and Silas beaten up and thrown in jail. They were delivered miraculously, and they went to Thessalonica. There was quite the success and the Jews stirred the people to accuse Paul and Silas of turning the place upside down. They then went to Berea where they were mostly intellectuals and

FAVORED ON PURPOSE

proved their gospel by searching the Scriptures. Here the people were turned against Paul, and he went on, leaving Silas and Timothy in Berea. It was time to go to Athens where Apostle Paul preached the famous sermon on Mars Hill. He then proceeded to Corinth where there was an impressive success, and he lived there for a year and a half. It was there he penned the book of 1 and 2 Thessalonians regarding the coming of the Lord. He then traveled to Cenchrea, Ephesus, Jerusalem, and went back to Antioch in Syria.

The third missionary journey began from Galatia through to Phrygia, visiting the churches he had planted at Lystra, Derbe, Iconium, and Pisidia. He then went to Ephesus where he stayed for three years. The idolatry ebbed and the silversmiths will run out of business, and they incited the people against the gospel, but Paul was proven innocent and released. He went back to Macedonia, then

FAVORED ON PURPOSE

Greece. He stayed at Corinth for three months. It was here he wrote the book of Romans, which is the most important book where he treated the salvation subject squarely.

The book of Romans is considered the greatest work done by Apostle Paul on the dynamics of salvation and what it really portends for the soul. The Roman church is not completely captured in history, but from Scriptural accounts, we see that the church became famous for her steadfast faith in Christ Jesus. He wrote to the Roman church for a variety of reasons.

Looking closely at the other books, it is so different from the book of Romans. Most of them were directed at addressing specific needs of the various churches, but the book of Romans is an epistle.

Apostle Paul needed assistance for his Spain trip. Again, he was impressed by the level and showing of their faith that he wrote in his capacity as an apostle to the Gentiles to establish and set things in order.

The unique impression Paul had of his office which filled him with so much zeal also contributes to make this book a wonder. It is arguably the best of all his letters. This is a church he neither founded nor preached to. This makes it more of an epistle than a letter. There is no prior mention of any teaching, and he assumes that they have been taught a number of things. He was more particular about building and making sure of a lot of things, and he does it in so systematic a format that it is difficult to fault.

Other reasons that could be adduced for this wonderful letter could be that he was preparing them to get ready for his visit to Rome, to carry on their faith and spread it to the Christian community in Rome. He was particular about the influence and potential of false teachers and what they could do to the flock. This letter was also aimed at securing them from people of such ilk, as well as resolving inner conflicts that could arise.

Paul begins his communication with the church in Rome with an exposition of the righteousness of God. He declared that he was not ashamed of the gospel as is the manner of some today. He called it The Power of God unto salvation. He harped on the transformative power of the gospel when applied to our lives, touching on the power it has to save any life, which cannot be compared to any other power in the universe to do such, and what is more, it is as free as the air we breathe, with no strings attached whatsoever. Whoever needed, it was his!

According to him, the just shall live by faith. As long as the just person expressed and exercises faith in Christ, salvation was his to enjoy, both here and in the hereafter.

FAVORED ON PURPOSE

There then comes the priority which seems to exude some streak of partiality, but it isn't so. It is according to the leadership of the Holy Spirit. It is to the Jew first, then the Gentile. This was because the Jews were the first to have the privilege of hearing the gospel before the Gentiles were engrafted in when they proved to be unworthy of such chance. It goes without saying that right from the word "go", the Jews were God's beloved and chosen people, and God has never hidden this fact through the years. Gentiles were predominantly idol worshippers and the number one problem the Jews had in copying their ways. Even when Christ came, he said he was sent to the lost sheep of the house of Israel. The Spirit was one, and the leadership was the same through the ages, and so Paul in his time could not do any more than going according to that leadership. He made a habit of visiting the Jews first to give them the opportunity. As a matter of fact, had the Jews not rejected the gospel at that point, I wonder if the Gentiles would have had any chance at the gospel whatsoever. But it would appear that it was all in the divinely ordained purpose of God for the Gentiles to have a shot at the gospel, therefore, the occasion had to be created for it to happen.

Next, we see the mode of righteousness God calls His own. It is so different in many ways from the brand of righteousness exclusive to man. This brand of righteousness is self-seeking, self-serving and legalistic on all fronts, and seeks to exalt the man. But all of this crumbles before the Lord, grossly deficient, to the level that it is addressed as filthy rags by the Lord. It would not cut it in any way, rather, the righteousness which is of Christ is advertised and encouraged to be received and applied.

FAVORED ON PURPOSE

In Romans 8, which is the core of the aim of this book, we are given a blow by blow account of how the flesh and the spirit stand and operate parallel to each other, not just that they are working at cross purposes, but they are constantly on each other's jugular, in a bid to gain dominance and sway over the vessel. But when salvation happens, the Spirit gets the upper hand and is able to subdue the flesh. It does not completely mean that everything concerning the flesh dies out completely, but the cheering news is that it is not business as usual for the flesh, in that there is a bridle on its lusts and cravings, to give the Spirit controlling influence.

That dominance that was occasioned by the presence of the Spirit of God now brings us into a new kind of fellowship with our God, our desires become heavenly, and the flesh loses its hold much of the way, and God is now able to minister to us in His own way. This will now become our passion and life, and everything about you takes a

godly inclination. This is not to say that there will not be

trials and tribulations as is bandied about by most bread

and butter preachers of today, *who equate Christianity with*

zero challenges, but the indisputable fact is that whatever

we pass through in this present life, our place in eternity is

assured. It is surprising where the notion came from that

because one as decided for the Lord, every trouble

automatically is swept away. There's no verse of the

Scripture that supports this postulation in the entire Bible.

As a matter of fact, the only assurance we have of the Lord

is HIS PRESENCE WITH US when we pass through

difficulties, not the complete absence of challenges. The

Bible says those who will live godly in this world must face

persecution. He himself with all His anointing and power

was persecuted; how much more we that are mere

followers and believers?

FAVORED ON PURPOSE

Indeed, nothing that the eyes have ever seen is comparable to the glory that has been prepared for the people who give their life to God's will here on earth; it does not matter what it is called. Like the Bible aptly puts it, it does not matter what it is that seemingly has the potential of drawing us away, it is not enough to separate us from that love, be it hunger, death, poverty, danger, shame, and name it. We are also assured of our place not just in destiny, but in God's divine program for the earth. There is a divinely scripted plan that God has for the world in general, but inside it, like a mathematical subset, there is a loving, purposeful divine arrangement that the Lord has for His children according to His sovereign power.

One of the most current proofs that everything happening on earth has been divinely foreordained is the fact that a 'psychic pig' has been able to predict the semifinalists of the 2018 soccer fiesta going on in Russia. This is because, in the spirit, things are settled before it plays out in the physical, and anyone with power enough, be it ungodly or godly, can latch on to that realm to have a peek at what is happening there, and it will be accurate. *But that is an example of a global script of world events*. It has little to do with those that God has called His own. Within that little enclave, there is also a divine plan and program of what the Lord means to achieve to his personal praise and glory. For example, there are very few of God's children that He will allow possessing a certain level of wealth in this world. This is to shield them from the obvious temptation and snare of this world's vanity and riches, and it is Scriptural. Children of God who are born again are in God's exclusive program and since they are destined to come back to Him, He is jealous and particular over the kind of life they live and the things He allows them to pass through. He pays committed attention to the trajectory of their lives and makes sure His pleasure is gloriously achieved.

Mind you, the Glory of God is not only on the positive alone as it concerns the individual. It was God's divine plan for Stephen to die by stoning, and become the first martyr, but that was the beginning of the conversion of Saul to Paul. A story is also told in Russia some years back about seven young believers who were caught by the Russian soldiers in the heat of the persecution of the church at that time. Refusing to recant their faith in Christ, they were to be executed by allowing them to freeze in the cold by the seashore. The soldier who was in charge of the execution gave them the final chance by placing seven felt jackets and a bottle of warm vodka and rum beside him and asked them for the final time to denounce their faith. The believers refused, and one by one, naked as they had been stripped, they froze to a silent and chilling death. But an interesting thing happened. As they made up their minds for the Lord, the soldier was able to see in a vision that each man had a crown waiting for him as his soul ascended directly upwards. But when it got to the last man, the angel who had the crown would ascend and descend, unsteady, as he watched his brethren meet their deaths. He had become unsure of his destination, and when the doubt rose in him, added to the biting cold, he shouted in a loud voice, 'I recant! I recant Christ!' and dove for the jackets and warming drinks.

But the soldier saw what was actually happening, and had been curious about what was capable of making these men lay down their lives. It was interesting, and he suddenly saw the angel beckoning to him, and in a swift moment, he tore off his jackets, threw away the glass of rum, and stripped himself bare. He shouted, 'I believe in Christ! I believe!' He jumped into the freezing water and breathed his last. The crown meant for the last man descended on his head

instantly. Thus, God has used that occasion not just to

substitute an unstable soul, but to win one more.

Chapter 2

BE CONFIDENT

The twenty-eighth verse of the book of Romans chapter 8 begins with the confidence of the believer which leads him to believe that nothing happens by chance or by happenstance. That chapter says that all things work together for good to them that love the Lord, and to them that are called according to His purpose.

It is instructive to understand the thought pattern the apostle Paul is expressing here. And this will we do when we consider the build-up to that statement. Who are the people that know, how they know, and all the questions that are congruent to that statement have to be appreciated well.

First, the people in this context that know are those who are in God's program, the saints, who have the Spirit of God, who are called out of the world and belong to the celestial body of Christ, who do not walk after the flesh, but the Spirit. Because the Spirit is in full sway and swing in the life of the believer, he or she is ignorant of what he or she needs unless the Spirit is piloting such requests, and keeping it in consonance with the timely dictates of the grand design and purpose of the Lord for the individual. The ignorance of what to pray for is a weakness made possible by the fall of man and advent of sin in the world. God cut off the connection of the physical with the Spiritual, and the plan of salvation was an attempt at restoring that connection, hence the desire of the man who is in Gods program to be a spiritual being.

FAVORED ON PURPOSE

With this confidence, the believer who is in God's program can now run along with the assurance that whatever he or she meets along the way, it will add up for good especially as he or she is able to identify his or her place in the body of Christ. The believer rests in the righteousness of the Almighty and in the childlike belief that there is no deception in the plan of God, neither is there any shadow of turning with Him, just like the famous songwriter said in "Great Is Thy Faithfulness."

That childlike confidence can be exemplified in the case of little Sharon who was skipping with her rope in the courtyard one Saturday morning. She had just finished her chores for the morning and was jumping gaily away, counting her jumps as the rope oscillated under her feet. She was in no mood to be disturbed and had looked forward to this part of her day every day and this was to be the most enjoyable part since there was not going to be

FAVORED ON PURPOSE

any schooling or calls from Mommy to do this or that: she

had made sure she tidied up everything that would evoke

the need for her attention. To make assurance a double

word, she has just peeped into her room and had

confirmed her mom sleeping soundly.

Ten, twenty, thirty skips and she began to miss the jumps.

The swinging was no longer falling in tandem with her lifts

and in the next three jumps she had fallen down and the

rope twisted in a certain fashion. Frustrated, she picked it

up and continued, determined to reach her 500-skip mark

that morning, but she had barely crossed the 100th skip

when the rope was completely tangled and mazed so much

that she could no longer use it. She sat on the floor for a

while, brooding, but it only lasted a record ten seconds. An

idea had struck her. She had a father.

As her footsteps approached the study where her father

spent most of his Saturdays consuming the dailies he

missed during the week due to his busy schedule, she heard voices. The tone looked serious and it sounded passionate, whatever they were discussing. She got there and offered her salutations, and left. It was Uncle Tim, and she knew better than interfere or interrupt those discussions which she could not make head or tail of. But she had no rope on her hand when she left. She had dropped it on her father's table.

An hour later, it was lunchtime and seated at the table with her mom and dad, she said, "Thank you Dad, for my rope."

'Which rope?'

Such is the childlike and faith with which God expects His children to trust Him with. The father didn't even know when he unknotted the rope for his daughter, but it was done alright- the child had implicit confidence that the father would solve her problem and got results. No wonder

FAVORED ON PURPOSE

God had to swear by Himself when Abraham went beyond the border in showing how far he could trust his God, sacrificing his only son. In the same way, the believer is expected to trust God's leading and navigation for his or her life, and the result would always turn out good, and that is what that book of Romans was trying to pass across.

Think of the many times we have faith in things we have no control over. We sleep. We have faith we would wake up the next day when we aren't even sure of the next breath. We sit on chairs confident that it will not collapse under our weight. Most of the time, it does not. We step out of our houses having faith we will come back, but the Bible says there is one step between life and death. In the end, we do come back.

The book of Romans is giving us a sure word of confidence here and we are expected to latch on to it and bet our lives on it. God's plan and life purpose for everyone must be achieved; and that without fail, with the cooperation of the individual or not. That is God's sovereignty.

In conclusion, children of God ought to rest their lives on God's promises without any atom of faltering. This is exactly what the devil hates and tends to fight in us, by facing us with a myriad of options as well as feeding us with examples of people who have trusted God and it 'failed' them. Because he is unaware of God's purposes and workings, he adjudges it a failure when someone goes through an extreme difficulty and maybe succumbs to it, forgetting that God can achieve His purpose in our lives even in death, which is the highest level of the misfortune. But to a Christian, the highest level of misfortune is eternal separation from Christ. For example, the purpose of God in sending His son Jesus Christ was one that entailed death; nothing else could cut it because the same Word said without shedding of blood there will be no remission of sin.

FAVORED ON PURPOSE

But the devil thought he had won when Christ breathed His last. In the end, we all know how it turned out.

Modern Christianity, courtesy of the same devil, has become commercialized and self-seeking, and as such, it has turned everyone into a critical mass of impatient and impenitent folk. But it was not so. The apostles of old esteemed their lives worthless as far as the gospel of Christ was concerned. Little wonder they surrendered themselves to the most gruesome of deaths for the gospel sake. This is because they were confident and resting on God's promises, knowing that they had not followed cunningly crafted fables of men according to the Scriptures. It should be so with us today, if not even more because we have a reference and a guide in the Scriptures.

Chapter 3

GOD IS STILL IN CONTROL

The thrust of this chapter is the phenomenon of all things working together for good for them that love God, and are called according to His purpose. Now, the emphasis should be on the definition of the word, 'all'. Simply put, it means all things, as long as English has not lost its meaning. All means all things. This is where the concept of predestination comes into play. A lot of scholars and leftists often have a quarrel with this concept, but there is a myriad of Scriptural verses that confirm this concept to be true. In the first place, even baring any Scriptural consultation, if we believe that the Almighty God is omniscient, omnipotent and omnipresent, then we should not have a hard time at all agreeing that He knows all things. If he knows all things, then no decision of man will shock him, till the end of the world. He knows exactly who will do what, who will believe in Him and who will not. By the way, all the activities and happenings on earth are the concepts of a well conjectured and scripted movie, and He controls all as He likes. It will be nice to get a concise overview of this concept because it is critical to understanding the thrust of this chapter.

WHAT IS PREDESTINATION?

The closest reference made to the concept of predestination and where in fact the word was mentioned is in Romans 8:28-30, which reads thus:

FAVORED ON PURPOSE

"Those whom he foreknew he also predestined to be conformed to the image of his Son, in order that he might be the firstborn among many brothers" (v. 29).

The definition of these terms aid everyday communication with ease and makes reference easier in the context of what is being said. It is always best to accurately and succinctly define a term that is in constant use, and a word such as this is so demanding of such an approach. It is important to define what predestination is to the layman for the better understanding of all and sundry. This is to give everyone a common frame or platform so we can well relate what we say.

The English word 'predestine' and predestination comes from the Greek term prorizo, which is a compound word that means, *"To determine beforehand or before time."* In effect, it means setting the ultimate destiny of a thing or a person before it was even made. This is a concept that applies to almost everything that happens in life and history, which is actually the way it is, but in Christian circles, much reference is made to it concerning salvation.

Essentially, the thrust of the concept of predestination is the fact that God has chosen our final destination long before we were born or even formed. It is true that some people have a big issue with this concept, but as long as the Scriptures are concerned, that is the final word on any subject as long as it has to do with Christianity. Christians believe that some have been destined by God for the pearly gates of heaven, while others have been also predestined for the fires and sufferings of the lake of fire. There are however differences on the basis of this foreknowledge. The question arises as to whether God looks into the future, and sees and knows who will respond to his call in the future, then slate that person for heaven, or does he handpick those who will believe Him, and as a result give them faith requisite for salvation? The former is seen as the Prescient view, while the latter school of thought is the Calvinistic view, famous for a notable reformer called John Calvin. According to those who agree with the prescient view, they postulate that the ultimate deciding factor is the individual, saying that God chooses the man for salvation only after deciphering how he or she will regard the gospel. The Calvinists make God the sole proprietor of the business of salvation. He determines from the beginning who will believe and who will not.

The people who are proponents of this prescient view are inclined to that passage in Romans 8 because since God predestinates those he knew would believe, He would also choose people for salvation that he knew from the beginning. But the problem is that the passage does not talk about those whom He foreknew would believe. The fact is that Paul the apostle was not talking about his knowledge of facts, but of how well He knows individuals. That in itself could be a way of differentiating the two schools of thought, however, hidden it is. God knows people not just on the surface, but intimately and when He chooses someone, He sets His love on him that drives him to heed the salvation call. Even though He knows what they will do, the concept of predestination here encompasses His love which He puts in the heart of the man, which spurs him on to receiving His Spirit and being glorified.

It is important to note at this juncture that the believer does not choose God; it is even absurd to imagine that possibility. God chose us and set His love upon us. He does not decide based on what we decide, but it is His elective love we respond to by believing in Him. If it were the other way round, there will be room for self-glorification and pride that tends towards boasting. We make the choice for the Lord because He chose us in the first place.

FAVORED ON PURPOSE

For the avoidance of doubt, all things in that Scriptural verse refers to any and everything that happens to the child of God. It does not matter what it is- good, bad, not so good, ugly-there is a divine purpose that is in the offing and in the process of playing out in the life of the believer. Indeed, nothing about the life of a child of God ever turns out bad in the final analysis-our limited sensibilities always convinces us of a contrary view especially when we see negativity dwelling for so long among children of God. Even among people who are not of the stock of the Lord, the phenomenon of change being the most constant thing applies to the core and is evidenced for everyone to see and agree with. But the difference is that while things seem rosy for them here, this is where their whole conversation ends, with a fearful and an unenviable hereafter waiting for them as long as they are not born again, but not a child of God, who has an eternal date with the Lord, to rule and reign with Him. As a matter of fact, because of the peculiar calling of children of God and how the devil hates them, they are often at the butt of pummeling's and afflictions of a variety of sorts from the devil, directly, and the world in general, because the world is an extension of the devil's spiritual kingdom. But the good news is that it has a limit and a certain timeline beyond which the devil or whatever malady it is, must not cross. This one is determined by the Almighty God Himself, and the devil has no say here whatsoever. This is quite evidenced in the converse that happened between the devil and God regarding the business mogul, Job. After waving him before the devil and accepting the challenge posed before him on account of the reason for his faithfulness, God accepted but placed a limit on where and what he could afflict. He was permitted to tamper with his finances, his health, his livestock, his posterity, and even his marriage, but there was a ban on his life. It was a no-go area for him. Left with the devil, he would have desired to make an end of him as he liked, but for the determinate counsel of God and what He intended to achieve in the life of His servant Job.

It is important to understand at this juncture that the devil was driven from a place where true Christians are destined for and that irreparably and irredeemably as well, and it will be foolhardy to expect to be treated lightly or kindly by him. As such, he seeks to fully exploit and explore every avenue he can to make life as miserable as he can for God's children, more like since their life in the hereafter is assured and rosy, he will do his best to frustrate them here on earth, and possibly drag as many as he can away to his final abode with him. But be that as it may, he is a spirit that was created by someone, and on that thankful premise, his reach and effect on the lives of God's children are defined and regulated. We all know how Job's suffered buffetings from the enemy and lost all that he had in one fell swoop, but when God was satisfied with his faith (which He was always confident of anyways) he made his former end a joke compared to what he became when the trial came to an end.

The Bible is so conveniently quoted or alluded out of context today that it is shocking the mindsets people carry about in the name of representing Christ. A lot of Bible truths are now completely quoted out of context or conveniently twisted to suit human lusts and ideas, and a part of this book of Romans 8 has also unfortunately fallen prey to this savage and unfortunate mutilation. Even though it has not been verbally quoted to general knowledge, it would appear that the verse was quoted to mean all things are good to those who love God, instead of **all things work together for good to those who love God and are called according to His purpose**. This is because a lot of people cannot reconcile the children of the God of heaven in His splendor and might being at the receiving end of afflictions and suffering. There is this overly grandiose view of God which is sensuous, fleshly and limited, and it is unfortunately propagated about in most facets of Christendom.

It is widely believed that once one is a child of God, he or she is now immune to all the sufferings and disadvantages of life, at the touch of a button. Even in the same Bible, there is actually precedence to this, but it is a gross misrepresentation of the personality of Jesus Christ, as well as his teachings and what is to be expected of those who toe His beaten path. The friends of Job could not imagine a man of the caliber of Job both in religious and financial circles, succumbing and rotten and pining away under severe illness and abject poverty. To them, there could have been no other explanation for this other than the fact that he was a secret sinner, and his sin had found him out and caught up with him. But Job was sure of himself and pleaded his innocence, and his latter end was more than a perfect vindication of his status with his Maker. This, in its own right, has given rise to the postulation of this super-health and super-wealth form of Christianity, which in actual and practical terms has no sound Biblical backing. As long as you decide for God, misfortune ceases to know your address, and it is all goodies and roses all the way. But the same Bible said that all of the people who will live godly will suffer persecution. *The only assurance that was promised was the grace to overcome, not the complete absence of trouble*. Jesus Christ who is the beginning and end of the Christian conversation was not only persecuted, he was crucified and killed in the most gruesome manner, not by strangers, but by His kinsmen. Elisha who was a force to reckon with in his day and age as a prophet died of common fever. Such is the actual truth of what we have signed up for, what we have promised in our lives to defend and promote. So all things add up, work together, for good to those who love God, and are called according to His purpose, not all things being good.

We are not in control of what comes our way in our estate as God's children, but through it all, whatever it is, good or bad, it will add up to the glorification of the Lord and our own good too in the end. The confidence that God is in full charge of the proceedings of our lives as His subjects should be overwhelming and implicit. That is the only way and mindset to have if we are to weather the storm, and not fall prey to the evil dazzle of the enemy at times when we become most vulnerable.

God is still in the business of extracting good out of evil; the enterprise of glorifying Himself from conditions that seem adverse. Again, the Bible being the most profound point of

FAVORED ON PURPOSE

reference and compass, there is sufficient precedence and backing to this fact. The story of Joseph most readily comes to mind to encapsulate and summarize the entire thought pattern of this book. This is because it contains everything that is needed to background all the points laid out here. First, there was a determined purpose for the life of Joseph which was to preserve life and help his people. Even that in itself was a part of the entire grand design because had the children of Israel not sojourned in the land of Egypt 400 years, there would have been no occasion to pull them out of the resulting bondage with a mighty hand. That aside, the end of the discourse was shown to Joseph in a dream, and he related it to his brothers. He was to rule over not just his house but his country. The exposition of the dream was the beginning point of the series of ugly incidents that was to unfold the ultimate aim of God for his life. Now his brothers were already jealous of him because he was the son of the woman Jacob their father really loved, and with the death of their mother Rachel, all the love changed base and alighted on Joseph and Benjamin. The dream aggravated things further, and before he could realize, he was on his way to the slave market, and he landed in the house of Potiphar. Because of his righteous stand, he was soon hurled into prison, where God's favor never deserted him. But when his time was ripe for God to be glorified in his life, a chain of events that was to announce him began to take place, and before you know what was happening, he was already the vice president of Egypt. What God intended to do happened to the letter in his life, and his part and role in the ultimate script were done from there.

As children of God, our belief system is that whatever the situation is, God is more than capable to bring good out of it, not just good in the collective sense, but the glory of God is paramount, and we through whom that glory is obtained stand to gain all the more if we just live our lives on this premise and allow God to take full course in our lives. As a matter of fact, all things that are good come out of things that are seemingly evil, fundamentally. If as God's children we are able to divorce our minds from the pressure and severity of the evil as it befalls, and focus our minds on the ultimate purpose of God concerning our lives, things will be much easier for us, and the pain of the misfortune will be easier to live with, with that confidence that God is sovereign and in full control of whatever comes our way.

- Why will God allow us to lose that loved one?

- What's God hoping to achieve, allowing you as a dedicated staff of a company to be sacked ignobly, out of no immediate fault of yours?

- Why will a lady who married as a virgin to a man she loves remain childless for years on end, whereas, her counterparts who have had more than their fair share of philandering and even abortions

before marriage procreate like rats?

These are some of the questions which make us sorrow

and even charge God foolishly at some point, but if we can

actually take time out to spiritually reflect on these things

with baseline of God's will to do what He likes with our

lives, things would be easier to handle, and not just that,

the end of it will be surely glorious. For starters, women

who were delayed before having children in the Scriptures

usually came out with generational prophets. The statistics

are there-from Samuel to John the Baptist to Joseph and

the rest of them. God can allow you to lose your loved one

so as to make you have a clearer picture of Him, and not to

idolize that person if He deciphers that the person is likely

to hamper your relationship with Him. I know of a woman

who only became a Christian after her husband died. The

husband was her all in all, her prayer mercenary, her go-to

machine for all things spiritual. Today that woman is a

darling daughter of God. God in His goodness CANNOT

punish His children except for sin and wrongdoing, and

even at that, it has never been a forever thing. Besides,

even in sin, whoever God employs to punish His children

will still face the wrath of God. He did it to

Nebuchadnezzar, even as it was His finger that

orchestrated the exiling of the children of Israel to Babylon

for their transgressions. Such is the depth of love God has

for His children, and it would be too condescending and

unheard of for Him to deliberately subject His children to

unnecessary suffering for no just cause. In essence,

whatever a child of God goes through is for his or her own

good; or there is an intrinsic aim to it which will manifest

sooner or later. The problem with man is sight and time;

most especially the time lag between the beginning of the

trial and the end of it. It was what Job's wife saw; how the sores had riddled his body beyond recognition, to the level he could not even put on clothes nor sleep on the bed, his groans of excruciating pain, and everything that came with his illness that made her feel it was better to curse God to His face and die, than continue in the condition, and she suggested it to him. But we all know the answer she got. Such is the power and influence that sight has over a man, and makes it difficult to believe that there can ever be respite, and provides ample platform for the ministrations of the enemy.

Another part of the passage in Romans 8 worth hammering on is the concluding phrase- **to them that love God and are called according to His purpose**. As it has been previously mentioned, there is a grand design for the world as a cosmos, but within that same scripting is a purpose specially crafted for those people who will believe in God, and their lives and all that happens to them has been jealously guarded by the Lord, for He cannot afford to leave them for a second, if that is even possible. These are the set of people that the devil is after with so much gumption; the people that are of such immense threat to his kingdom and given the split chance, he would waste no time in making mincemeat of them. The jealousy of them acquiring what he could not get, eternal life, would spur him on to doing all he can to frustrate, impoverish, demean, mock, persecute and even physically harm them. His best moment are those times when there is a program God wants to accomplish in their lives and God allows him access to their lives, but for a season. That is when he brings his full arsenal of evil upon them, knowing he might never get this chance again, and rains it down with gusto, as was the case with Job. But, the thing here is that it only happened for a season, and he was restored to twice who he was in the beginning. What God wanted to prove was to nullify Satan's claim that Job only served Him because God blessed him and made him wealthy. God was able to make it abundantly clear to the enemy that no condition whatsoever was capable of making Job curse God or offend him deliberately, and that ended the argument, while Job continued enjoying his life till he died at a ripe old age. There could have been no more attacks from the enemy.

It would appear actually that more and more of God's children go through misfortune statistically speaking, but it is not actually the case. The issue is that because of the way the world is fashioned, with Satan at the complete helm of affairs, there is this subtle effort towards magnifying and giving negative coloration to everything called godliness and righteous living. It is made to seem

- Insipid
- Boring

FAVORED ON PURPOSE

- Full of disadvantage

- Bereft of benefit

- Synonymous with poverty and mediocrity, and the likes.

The result is that it is mostly made so unattractive and people will rather take the easy, frictionless path that will land them in an inevitable doom. But that does not in any way mean that even in the wrong life it is all rosy; it is not. They go through some misfortune too, and the sad part is that because they are under Satan's jurisdiction, he gets to dictate what happens and when it happens, and how their end will be like. Additionally, because there is nothing like mercy in his dictionary, he gets to have his fill doing as he likes.

Like has been previously mentioned, and is aptly stated in that verse, God loves His children first, and that love makes them love Him back. 'Those that love God' in that context means those whom the love of the Father has drawn to Himself. As such, those that love God and are called according to His purpose are the people who are the owners of this promise. Nothing can ever happen to them except what God has ordained, and the ultimate aim here is for their own good.

God's eternal purpose includes calling to salvation a people for Himself. In the book of 2 Timothy, Paul opines that God "has saved us and called us with a holy calling, not according to our works, but according to His own purpose and grace which was granted us in Christ Jesus for all eternity." Here, Paul calls those for whom these things are meant for and accurately defines them, and clearly as well to mean those who love God. The distinction is clear and understood.

FAVORED ON PURPOSE

It is important to understand here that while it would seem that the verse there is a good ground for universal optimism; this verse has some dividing line. If you hate God and you are not in His divine program for His children, all things will NOT work together for good for you. Possibly some things and temporarily too, but never all things. God's provisions in that verse are strictly for the people whom His elective love has drawn to Himself. There are two approaches to this description of this set of people.

1. Those People for whom all things work together for good for most of essence love God.

This can be seen as the human side of the balance even though it has God's driving force behind it. Like earlier mentioned, none of us would love the Lord outside of his initial and elective love for us. When the gospel first came to us telling us of God's profound love for us, to the level of sacrificing His beloved son, promising eternal life to those who will believe in Him, we responded in that faith to reciprocate that love. The transforming power of the love of God changed our hearts from being inimical towards God and His attributes and put the desire in us to please Him. We love Him now as it were.

Important to note here also is the fact that loving God as portrayed in Romans 8 is a condition and not a description. It is a condition that shows God's elective love for us, and not one that is dependent on our love for God per time. It does not say that as long as you love God you will access this verse, but when your love for Him grows lukewarm or cold, you cease to enjoy the benefits. Granted, there are times when our love for God may require strengthening or reviving, it can never be divorced from the life of the Christian that he or she loves God. It is a description of what God has sealed and cemented in the life of the Christian, not so much what he or she does or doesn't do.

FAVORED ON PURPOSE

There are three other places where Paul mentions our love for God, in 1Corithians 2:9, 8:3 and Ephesians 6:24. The question now is, since it is entirely what God has done for the believer, why does he mention it? He did so because of the pressure and things that come up when trials are at its peak. At such times, it is important for us to affirm and reconfirm our love for the Lord despite what we go through. Like said previously, these are times when the devil is at his deceiving best, because of the vulnerability of our status at times like this. It is at times like this we need to not just be reminded, but to remind ourselves that the Lord is our chief treasure and that He paid the supreme sacrifice for our sins.

Again, when there is persecution, it is time to drum it into our sensibilities that the love of God and our love for Him is one thing that can never be taken from us, even as our material possessions can go in the twinkling of an eye, as was the case with Job. Our bodies physically can be

subjected to all forms of depravity and torture, but not our

chiefest possession, the love of God in our hearts. The

Psalmist rightly expresses this thought in Psalms 73 when

he says,

'Who have I in heaven but thee? Beside you, I desire nothing

on earth. My flesh and heart may fail, but God is the

strength of my heart and my portion forever.'

So in essence, as long as you have tasted how sweet the

love of God is through the gospel, all things work together

for your good.

2. The people for whom all things work together for
   good are called according to Gods purpose. They
   are in His plan.

This is the same people whom God refers to as the same

people that love Him but are referred to from God's

viewpoint. This is so that no one will feel that his or her

FAVORED ON PURPOSE

love for God emanates from himself or herself, or that it is the primary thing, the emphasis is on the love of God that engineers the believer's love. Bishop Moule captures it perfectly when he says that *"not one link of the actual Redemption chain is our forging else the whole chain would indeed be fragile."*

When we see the word "call or calling" in the New Testament epistles, it is referring to God's effectual call which caters to His purpose. According to the definition of the Westminister Shorter Catechism, effectual calling is the work of God's Spirit, whereby, convincing us of who we are in our sinfulness and misery, enlighten our minds and changes it from the carnality to the knowledge of Christ, and inclining our will to Him, and persuading us to embrace the Jesus freely offered to us in the gospel. In effectual calling, God does not force us against our will, but freely, which is actually something made possible by the grace He has given us.

The most potent evidence of God's calling in our lives is the hearing and effectual belief of the gospel, and agreeing with its power to transform our lives, and heart. The gospel of salvation thus believed, makes its entry and changes the will and desire. The believer now cares for the Bible and treasures it above any other book and agrees to its position as final in his or her life. There is no more excuse made for sin and no more love for it, and in its place, there is the desire to fight it and kill it, with all hate and detest. Anyone who has this testimony surely has all things working together for good for him or her. _But that does not mean that when tragedies happen in our lives, it is to be seen as good._ Painful as it is, the issue is that there is a good purpose and end to it.

FAVORED ON PURPOSE

God has planned an eternal good and advantage for those He calls to the salvation of their souls. Now all things here includes, for clarity sake, the good things that God gives us (it cannot be bad all at one season and good in ten years' time) as well as what the book of Romans calls "the suffering of this present time" encompassing hunger, danger, death, persecution, sickness, natural disasters, accidents, war, plane crashes, problems at work, traffic jams, relationship issues, even car misbehavior.

One is also tempted to ask if it also precludes when we sin against God. It applies, in that sin is too small a factor to hinder God's purpose for our lives, which is sanctification and glorification. This, however, will not go without a caveat. When we sin with the impression that God will work on it for our greater good, it is counterproductive. It goes without saying the God is not mocked, and there will be dire consequences for wrongdoing.

FAVORED ON PURPOSE

Does it make us any less of God's children? The answer is an emphatic No! David was a man after God's heart, as God confirmed, but when he sinned with Bathsheba and set him up to be killed, not only was his kingdom under severe threat, he lost four sons in his lifetime. God can use our sin to show us how untrustworthy our efforts at pleasing Him are if we truly turn around and repent of our sins. The same treatment was meted out to Peter after denying Christ thrice.

That being made clear, evil is evil of itself. It is not good, but it is painful and hard. It is grieving to lose a loved one. Misfortunes of life are a pain on the flesh and spirit. It should be seen for what it is: evil and completely bad, as well as difficult to cope with. When we are delayed certain things, not only are we at a disadvantage, it makes us susceptible to tantrums and taunts from adversaries and detractors, especially those who are in the know of our

FAVORED ON PURPOSE

relationship with God, sometimes even fellow brothers and sisters in Christ who lace advice with taunts on account of our situation. But in God's gracious program, He will always fashion out a way of working these discouraging situations out for our good as we submit to his super knowledge and guidance. He makes sure we see His hand and love in ways we would not have realized had it not happened. In the end, our faith and trust in Him are solidified. This is all for our ultimate good, which is to mold us to the image of Jesus Christ, who according to the Bible learned obedience through the things He suffered. In summary, it is possible that good and bad are citizens of this world, but we have a consolation that an incomparable glory awaits us in the hereafter.

This knowledge of God working things together for our good ought to bring us reprieve and comfort when trials peak. It is so refreshing that we see Paul being abundantly sure of what he was saying, and not from a place of hope or feeling. He does not say "we hope" or "we feel'" but rather "we know." This is because God isn't an idle God that does things out of chance or probability, but He is deliberate in the things He says and does, or allows happening. The long and short of it is that He has predestinated us to conform to the image of His son, and nothing can derail that purpose.

Some people hold the view that the teaching of God's sovereign election is not fit for general consumption because it seeks to divide, and it does not seem practicable, but God did not cause Paul to write it so as to upset us, but to get to know Him deeper. This fact is one that is hugely practical and is brought to bear best when we are faced with difficult situations. The underlying truth here is that God will use it to ultimately shape one into the image of Jesus Christ, no matter what it is. It is even more disheartening to think that we are worshipping a God who has no control over world affairs, and who is just allowing happenstance to play out. It is even scarier to think that way.

ELLA

Ella had met Randy in the most unusual of circumstances. She was not one who paid strangers heed, but there was something about this dashing young man that she could not just seem to shrug off that evening as she caught him staring at her at the mall. It would seem that both of them saw something fixating about each other, for long after they both realized they were staring at themselves, the same electrifying force had continued the renewed mutual interest for a few more seconds. She could not complain about his rudeness, he could not reject how peaceful and serene she appeared. Finally, after what seemed like a generation, they were able to extricate themselves from each other's ocular grip, Ella almost dropping the can of sardines she had found interest in, but her Adonis was to the rescue. He had leaped ten steps to where she stood, and the can did not touched the floor and attracted unnecessary attention, to the relief of the both of them. Without a word, contacts had been exchanged; there was no need for any verbal exchange. The attraction was not just powerful, but mutual. They had agreed to meet again a few days later at a restaurant of her choosing.

They meet on a cool Friday evening after the hassles of work had cemented everything and allayed every fear of wining and dining with a complete stranger. He was not only breathtakingly handsome; he was full of good manners and etiquette. Appearance wise, he was everything she looked forward to, and he loved cats and books like she did. Most of the evening was spent discussing books they

FAVORED ON PURPOSE

had mutually read, the characters and some of their work that had made headlines, and when two hours into the date they realized they had hardly touched what they ordered, they were relieved and overjoyed at how well they synced. It ended on a convivial note, and Ella felt she had known him all her life.

Now Ella had had her fair share of heartbreaks, and she had decided to take some time off the dating scene to pick herself up, and Randy was such a breath of fresh air. Not only was he young and fresh, he had all the airs of a responsible man, working at one of the country's foremost multinational firms. She was so drawn to him, and from that day, not two hours passed without some form of exchange between them online. She was looking to get married to him, and something akin to a relationship had started. When he invited him to some family dinner, all he did was to win the hearts of his parent and siblings in a way only he knew how to. Her mother would steal conspiratorial winks at her, applauding the wonderful choice she had made, while her father would go on and on with him about business and the politics of their day until the teens who were her siblings would be completely edged out of the conversation. When it came to literature, politics, business, investment, touring, name it, he always had not just something to say, he had something tangible to say which showed how much he had read and knew about the field of endeavor. The evening had ended with her dad hugging him tightly, something he had never done to any of the men who had been gracious enough to follow her home.

The chemistry had become stronger and stronger as the days went by, and life could not have been any better for Ella who could not believe her luck. As a Christian, she did not believe in luck but felt this was God's way of recompensing her for all of those failed relationships and heartbreaks she had suffered in the past. The way they had met even lent enough credence to that fact. He had just appeared from nowhere, and they had jelled. As such, she did not bother committing him into her Maker's hands for direction. Things had happened so fast, and in two months she was wearing his engagement ring.

Then, one day, it happened.

"It's not you."

"Honey, it's me."

"I feel I am not worthy of such an angel as you. You deserve better. You deserve a man who would treat you better than I am treating you. Please understand how hard it is for me to do this dear. Am sorry I can't marry you anymore."When she revived in the hospital to the relieved gasps from her parents and relations, another bout of wild crying resumed.

FAVORED ON PURPOSE

So she had lost Randy! What would her life be like from here? It was better she took her life there and then, this instant! The heartbreak was too much!

She lunged forward to the first aid kit just above her bed, and in seconds, a bottle of rubbing alcohol was in her hands, making way to her mouth, but a swift move from her brother knocked the bottle from her hand spilling its contents on the bed, and making her struggle with him to retrieve the bottle.

'Ella, look!'

It was Randy, on the television screen. He had just been arrested by the police for battering and killing his wife. He was being led away handcuffed, from his apartment, a different one from where he told her he lived.

Her tears dried instantly.

"I want to go home."

FAVORED ON PURPOSE

Chapter 4

THE FAVOUR

This would be more of a summary chapter to encapsulate all that has been previously outlined in the book before now. For clarity's sake, there is need to emphasize the fact that Paul did not say that all things are made good by God; this would be undermining His sovereignty and giving a totally wrong impression of all the Scripture stands for. Unfortunate incidents can happen, in fact, they do happen, but the thing about it is that they all add up for us to see the greater good that is in the foreseeable picture. Ella was dating someone that was so agreeable to her and she felt she had found an angel in human skin. Then the bombshell that struck her when out of his volition and from nowhere, her fiancée decided to suspend further dealings with her, and she was on the verge of committing a grieving suicide. But God who was rich in mercy decided to show her what she would have entered into had they continued, much as she would have wanted. The man was not only previously married, everything about him was a lie, and he was an abuser, to the level of murdering his wife in such a manner. Had she continued with him that would be her fate as well, apart from the shocking discoveries that would befall her. Knowing this, she had no other choice but to pick herself up and appreciate God who prevented this from happening, despite her negligence of Him.

Such is the way our loving Father deals with His children. His will is never for us to needlessly suffer pain, but whenever it happens or He allows it to come our way, there is a part of Him He wants us to see that we are not previously aware of, and when we see it, we cannot but glorify Him for His watchfulness and faithfulness towards us.

As long as one is a believer in Christ, he or she is a part of this glorious and interesting program. You go through the rigors, but you see the reason it is happening. Sometimes, it is not compulsory God actually lets us see the reason everything happens to us. That is the truth of the matter. Sometimes, allowing us to see the reason behind certain things that happen is as a result of His foreknowledge and consuming love, but at other times, he may decide not to explain anything or show anything. The truth of the matter is that in actual fact, He does not owe us any explanation; our love and trust for Him and in Him to give us the best in all our dealings with Him should suffice. If we agree that He is sovereign and His decision is final in our lives, then this should not be such a hard nut to swallow. But if we believe that we have other options, then it becomes a problem accepting this fact.

At a time God told one of His prophets to take a trip to the potter's workplace, to show him how the potter handles the work of his hands. The prophet was able to see how the clay yielded to every touch of the potter and aligned itself with everything that suited the mind of the potter. The purification process of the potter was of interest, how the potter would sift through the volume of the clay searching for impurities because these things would hamper the yield of the clay in forming whatever shape the potter had in mind. It would also become a weak link and make the resulting shape brittle an easy to break when it was eventually formed. Such becomes the care and discipline of the potter that makes him knead the clay not with a machine but with his hands, to be sure that there is no impurity like sand or wood or stones that are not needed, and the moment any of these things are found, it is thrown out of the mix instantly. This continues until a free, pure mass of clay is arrived at. Next is the molding process. The potter molds and forms and creates until he is satisfied. Sometimes he molds to a certain shape, only to collapse everything and begin afresh, trying to create a completely different thing from what he started out with. In all of this, the clay never protested or asked the potter what it was doing. God then likened the entire scenario to His relationship with His beloved, Israel.

The burden of trust in God is really proved in times like this. God expects His children to have unwavering trust in Him, and for it to transcend verbal affirmations, to practical obedience and submission. The notion that everything that happens to us as children of God is for our own good should be uppermost in our minds and sensibilities. Where God proffers an explanation, we take and thank Him, where

FAVORED ON PURPOSE

He does not, we also forge ahead, thanking Him as well,

knowing that He can never lead us astray. Such should be

the mind-set we should operate with as children of God.

The underlying thought here is that God does not do good

or evil, He rather allows good or evil to happen to us, but

we can be rest assured that out of everything, good will be

the product. The Bible says that every good and perfect gift

comes from the Lord. The deciding factor of enjoying this

interesting side of God is if we are His children. As long as

were in that bracket, we can be sure of His unfailing love

that will bring good out of all happenings to us.

There is a part of the program of God called the permissive

will of God. Inside of God's provided will, other things can

come in between but ultimately, there will most

importantly come what God wants to achieve. The

permissive will of God can either be positive or negative,

but in the midst of it, God's ultimate purpose will be

brought to the limelight, and the beauty and appropriateness of it bared for all to see and appreciate. For example, by the right of the covenant, the ruler ship of the children of Israel was to be ceded to the tribe of Judah. It was to be so according to the charge given to the children of Jacob which later represented the twelve tribes of Israel. Along the line, the children of Israel became yoked with the bondage of slavery in the land of Egypt. They cried to God and God sent Moses to deliver them with a mighty hand. Along their journeying on the route to the Promised Land, they met many nations which they were commanded not to pattern their lives after. But in the course of time, they became attracted to the ways of the nations they interacted with and saw the logic in their style of kingship. Before long, they started making calls and demands for a king according to what they were used to. The prophetic style of leadership which God gave to them

FAVORED ON PURPOSE

in the person of Prophet Samuel became boring and

unattractive to them and they began to crave for secular

leadership. Before long, the protests and demands had

reached a deafening volume and Samuel cried out to God

for direction on what to do so that he would not be

mobbed one day. God gave him leave to anoint a man

whom the people wanted, qualified in every physical sense,

tall, articulate and a people pleaser, charismatic in all that

was required. But he was from the tribe of Benjamin, Saul

by name. By this time the lust for what they wanted had

made the children of Israel forget the original charge and

what was the template for God's mind concerning them.

The king was not from the tribe of Judah, but he was

crowned anyways. The people had had their way; they had

taken their place in the comity of nations as acceptable and

agreeable. They had a king according to how they wanted it

and had a standing like other nations, and God had

permitted it. But what followed and the ignoble way Saul spent his life throughout his stint as king of Israel showed how foolhardy it was to circumvent God's will, as all of them came to realize and even testify. And when David who was actually God's intention eventually arrived, it was clear to the people what the difference was between the permissive will of the Lord and His eternal will concerning man.

First, Saul's rulership was never a spiritual one. This was never God's plan for Israel. Administratively, he had it, but when it concerned his relationship with God, it was a wobbly one. He always had an excuse for his wrongdoing. He would not obey the Word of God to the letter. He was sensuous, self-willed and full of himself. When it was time to slaughter the Amalekites, the instruction was to annihilate every breathing thing but he spared the fat cows and even the king's family whom he had made a league with and would have paid for it, if not for the timely

intervention of the Prophet, Samuel. Even at that, the wife

of the king escaped and was pregnant at that time. Little

wonder the son she bore became the great ancestor of the

wicked Haman, who grew up with incensed hatred for the

Jews in the time of Esther, and God also handled him in his

own perfect manner. But the truth is that had Saul obeyed

that command, Israel would have been spared one less of

an enemy in years to come. By the way, it was this singular

act that made God grow weary of Saul and decided to

extricate the kingdom from him. Even when David

appeared on the scene as the chosen of God, Saul's

treatment of him was one fuelled by jealousy and gross

insecurity, Things fell way south for him when he began to

employ the services of diviners and mediums which was a

gross sin and an indication of God's gross departure from

him. In essence, the people wanted their will which was

contrary to God's. He allowed them to have their way, and in the midst of it, to see how different and imperfect man's will is for the perfect will of God.

When God's will for a man is at play, it is like a round peg in a round hole; *so appropriate.* There is no need for struggles and worries of how things would be; the Lord makes things right when it should be. When a man is in God's perfect will, his protection is assured, God takes his security as his paid job. This is so different from the permissive will of God, which is always full of missed steps and wrong footings. The disadvantage is always glaring and the potential of God for that man may be delayed. It is never so with the man in the will of God.

But the cheering news is that in it all and through it all, God aims to bring out his ultimate good from every situation, even his permissive will. When the era of Saul was over, the people saw for themselves how different it was between a

FAVORED ON PURPOSE

God-ordained king and one they chose for themselves. At a point in Saul's rule, because he did not have the revelation of what it took to be a warlord as well as a ruler, he forced them to go on a fast before the war. They would have been killed in the war had his son Jonathan not disobeyed that command. Such was the clear lack of vision and stoic that Saul exhibited, and the people despised him even though they feared the throne. But not so with David, who was meek, humble and a man after God's heart.

At a time, he needed water from a certain well and no sooner had the words come from his mouth to no person in particular, when three of his henchmen went there at great risk to their lives and fetched the water for him. Even at that, David refused to drink of that water when they brought it. Such was the love and regard the people had for him during his time, but the reverse was the case for Saul.

FAVORED ON PURPOSE

By making man a free moral agent and giving him the power of choice, God has realized that while exercising that power of choice, it is possible for man to want to go his own way contrary to God's plan. In such cases, a provision, even if limited, would be accommodated. This proves to be the difference between what He would have preferred for the individual, as against what He just allows to happen.

It is important to note that there is a marked distinction between these two definitions. Make no mistake, we are obligated to obey the Lord, and aligning with His perfect will is the surest path to the niceties He has in store for us. But God knows we have the inclination to go our ways and may excuse our deficiencies to give us an alternative, so to speak, but which difference would be glaring to us in the end. But it should be noted that choosing our own way always comes with a price. Instances of the Perfect will of God and His permissive will include the following:

FAVORED ON PURPOSE

A. In a family arrangement, God's perfect will is one man, one wife. In Genesis 2:24, it says, "a man will leave his father and mother, and they will become one flesh." But in the permissive will, like in Deuteronomy 21:15, it says, "If a man has two wives..." suggesting that polygamy may be allowed.

B. In the same vein, when a family is breaking up, God's perfect will is that a man stays with his wife till death. Genesis 2:24 says a man will leave his father and mother and unite with his wife, to become one flesh. But in Deuteronomy 24:1, it says, "If a man marries a woman who becomes displeasing to him, he may write a bill of divorce and put her away."

C. Eating preferences

God's perfect will was vegetarianism, as shown in Gen 1:29 which says, "I will give you every seed-bearing plant on the

FAVORED ON PURPOSE

face of the earth and every tree that has fruit in it. But we see God's permissive will of favorism according to Genesis 9:3 which say, "Everything that lives and moves will be food for you." Just as I gave you green plants, I now give you everything.

* * *

In the political scheme of Israel, God's perfect will was the destruction of the Canaanites, according to Deut. 7:2a, which says, "When the Lord delivers them before you and you defeat them, you shall utterly destroy them." But we see God's permissive will in sparing the Canaanites thus in Judges 2:23 where it says that the Lord had allowed the nations to remain, he did not drive them out at once by giving them into the hand of Joshua.

Also, in the eternal destination of man, God's perfect will was the innocence of man, as in Genesis 2:25 where it says the man and the woman were both naked and they had no shame. But man sinned and fell into the permissive will of God and everything about him changed, according to Genesis 3:7 where it says the eyes of the both of them were opened and they realized they were both naked and sewed fig leaves for themselves.

But there are some who would argue that the permissive will of God is just a way of garnishing disobedience. It's just a way of cushioning the effect and weight of their sin and reducing it to just a number of options laid before us of which we are free to choose. In truth, the children of God suffered more under the rulership of Saul, who was NEVER God's choice for them. They wanted a king like other nations, without taking time to even investigate how the people were faring under such kind of rulership. At any rate, they wanted a king they could relate with, see, talk to, share ideas with, and so on. Plausible as it was, it was still

FAVORED ON PURPOSE

NOT God's mind for them, and they suffered the

consequences.

Similarly, the mind of God for them when He delivered

them from the bondage of Egypt was a journey of a

maximum of 40 days. But because of their sin and

disobedience, one day became one year, until they spent

40 years still en route the Promised Land. In essence,

permissive will should be seen as the seemingly negative

things that God allows to come our way in order to bring

forth a greater good, and not as if God permitted us to

disobey Him and get away with it. It is important this

distinction is made so that we do not get the wrong ideas

on this subject. We can lose a loved one so that the person

can go home to be with the Lord to rest if the ailment is

keeping the person in a vegetative state and sapping

relations and family of scarce resources. It is a seeming evil

with the greater good of saving the family pain and waste.

FAVORED ON PURPOSE

A story was once told of a world-renowned evangelist who preached to many and featured in many crusades where a lot of lives were turned to Christ. He moved mountains and brought terror to the kingdom of darkness. Yet God allowed him to be very poor, so poor at a time in his life that he could hardly feed. One day, in the heat and pressure of neediness and lack, he decided to spite the Lord to His face. He ordered a boy to go get him a shot of dark rum to calm his nerves. The boy said he would rather die than to add aiding and abetting this kind of sin to the list of his iniquities. He said he would not be the one to buy alcohol for a man of God, that he had his own wrongs to deal with. Now, the preacher after persuading the boy to no avail went to a liquor store in another part of the town where he felt no one knew him, bought the drink, and proceeded to the privacy of his house to down it. Instead of having a hangover the following morning, he was found dead, when repeated knocks on his door received no answer.

Painful as His death was to his family and friends as well as the general body of Christ, it was still a gain to the Lord because who knows, he might not go to hell. Yes, he died sinning, but the Lord was more interested in securing His investment in his life, in making him not to reproach His name, than any other consideration. God's ways are past finding out, and we can only refer to the things we can see and understand.

There is a superimposing precedence in all of this. This is the Ministry of God in the flesh, the Lord Jesus Christ. Now, from the beginning, God's own law said that without the shedding of blood there will be no remission for sin. Besides, whoever wanted to redeem someone according to the law had to have a relationship with him, a kinsman redeemer.

FAVORED ON PURPOSE

Now, no other blood of anyone who came through the process of sexual relations was qualified enough for that process. It had to be pure, untainted blood, innocent as they come. Thus, God decided to put on flesh to become a man. In that manner, he had an innocent blood which did not require fertilization by human processes, and since he put on flesh like man, he was now our kinsman, to see what we see, feel what we feel, and experience life like us.

At great expense and inconvenience to God, he made this sacrifice. Very few people understand the great condescension of having your own creatures crucify you, spit in your face, call you names and mock you. This is apart from the sacrifice of compressing a spirit larger than the entire universe into one smallish, lithe frame for this purpose. Great as this sacrifice is, costly as it is, it had to be done or else mankind would be doomed forever. When Jesus died, it was at a great cost and seeming loss not just to his friends, but nature as well. The earth revolted and cried out in protest. Earthquakes happened and thunder boomed. Their creator was being humiliated!

But it was more of an investment rather than a loss. A greater good was about to be birthed, at the behest of that death. As soon as the Roman spear pierced his side to ascertain the fact that he was truly dead, three things came out-the blood, water, and a third invisible one-His Spirit, which is indwelling in millions and millions of genuine born-again Christians and giving them the power to live lives that mimicked His own while on earth. Little wonder in Antioch they got the name Christians, because of the way they conducted themselves. Today, that spirit is still alive and active in the lives of believers of Christ, working His work and making a distinction between the world and the true church.

FAVORED ON PURPOSE

Following from this, if God did not find it difficult to bring good out of the evil of allowing His son to die for us, then it ought not to be weighty to us when seeming evil befalls us. The trust should be there that there is a greater good that is being aimed at and will manifest in due course.

But as believers, God gives us the favor to enable us to get through the thing we go through by His grace. When we believe in God, He equips us with the commensurate faith in Him to trust Him and the favor which is uncommon for us to overcome the pain of what we pass through, and not to succumb to it like people who have no hope in the outside world. God favors us so that the trouble and trials will not overcome us, and to see the good in the need for us to go through such trials as well.

***

FAVORED ON PURPOSE

As a child, it was difficult to know my father and my mom parted ways in a divorce. It was such a traumatizing period for me to watch two parents I had grown some way with separate in such a manner. Before long, my father developed heart trouble. I was about ten at the time, and I was pretty smart for my age. I knew what heart attack was, and I knew what was caused by putting the heart through much workload and stress. The reason for the stress was not lost on me as well, and in my mind it was not far from the fact that my mother remarried and went on with her life. I felt my mother was responsible for my father's death, and even though I lived with my mother, I began to resent her for this reason, and only God knows the extent to which that feeling could have taken me.

But thanks to the grace of God, I was able to let go of the pain and hurt it caused me and strike a loving relationship with my mom once more. I was even able to minister the gospel to her, and today she is a member of my church. At that time, because of the absence of my father, a lot of things could have gone wrong with my life. But God favored me and was able to show me the sunny side of things, to bring out the good out of a seemingly painful experience. This is an excerpt from a part of my personal life that buttresses the entire point of this book.

Conclusion

Our lives are a scripted text which has been summarily written by the Almighty God according to His omniscience. We live every fraction of our lives according to His purpose. Everything that pans out in our lives works out His divine aim for our lives.

The book of Romans chapter 8 does complete justice to this subject in bringing out this point. It chronicles the background of this book of Romans as well as what informs its recording and for what purpose. Indeed, Apostle Paul appears to be the most appropriate material for the job, being that he also had a painful part of his conversion, but which worked out for the entire good of the glory of God and the generality of the body of Christ, even up till this day

FAVORED ON PURPOSE

and as many as will believe, even tomorrow, until God's kingdom is established. The book of Romans backgrounds, explains and encapsulates this subject as well as other allied matters like establishing the power of God in the gospel, why it had to follow a certain racial trajectory, of course, according to the working and leading of the Holy Spirit.

We are enjoined to be confident of the workings of the grace of God in our lives and have implicit trust and faith in whatever God allows to come our way. Like a candle in the wind, we are to bow to whatever direction the wind of life may blow us as long as it is in consonance with the will and word of God. We exhibit this confidence mindlessly in our everyday affairs, so why is it that difficult to exhibit this when it comes to God's program for our lives? It is a food for thought that everyone ought to engage in and have a rethink. It does not take anything for us to balance our

114

weight on a chair, regardless of how capable it is to carry our weight, and in actual fact, it does. But there is a God that made that chair, yet we grumble when trusting Him becomes the subject.

But be that as it may, God is still in control, much as we would rather want to disbelieve. To the child of God and those called according to the purpose of God, it does not matter what happens to him or her or what the person goes through. There is a good and ultimate part of it that God wants to bring to the individual's notice, and it would be nice if it was focused on and seen. The emphasis, still, is on believers, for those are the select group of people to whom this promise specifically applies.

The favorite part of the mix is where God grants the platform for the believer to come out of his seeming misfortune better and bigger and wiser. It is adjudged a favor because something smaller or commensurate will cause dire consequences on some other person who is not a believer, but with children of God, the matter affects them differently. They see the hand of God in everything and go about their lives thanking Him and expecting the best. That is what God is trying to work out, and thus, he gave us to the image of His Son.

Besides the icing of the favor which comes as explained in the latter part of this piece, the thrust of this message is to get people to surrender to God. Once this happens, every other package is activated, and God becomes the sole architect and defender of your life, along with the other fringe benefits.

Made in the USA
Columbia, SC
30 July 2018